SUNRISE

*"Out of the darkness shines
a glimmer of light."*

STEPHEN SELBY

Cover photograph courtesy of Keri Hutchinson

ISBN: 9798387143991

PublishNation
www.publishnation.co.uk

Sunrise is a collection of poems telling the story of a journey through life, through good times and bad. Inspired by a love of nature and open water swimming, *Sunrise* shows that, through the power of friendship, we can triumph over adversity and find ourselves in a better place. *Sunrise* doesn't shy away from visiting some very dark places, but by understanding and accepting our own limits, our own mortality and embracing life, we can overcome these and savour the beauty and joy of the world around us. With plenty of humour, a bit of politics and a lot of swimming, *Sunrise* is ultimately a celebration of life, showing we can start afresh when the sun rises in the morning sky.

CONTENTS

INTRODUCTION

My grandmother was a keen open water swimmer in the 1930s before the war. Open water swimming was a very big thing in the 1920s and 1930s, almost exclusively with women. My grandmother was great friends with the legendary Gertrude Higginbottom, who was most famous for swimming from Ladye Bay to Clevedon Pier with the much missed Queen Elizabeth II. We will be hearing more from Gertrude later.

My grandmother was also great friends with Kathleen Thomas (the first person to swim the Bristol Channel), Edith Parnell and Gertrude Ederle. All of these brave women were inspired by the story of Betty and Mildred who were the first women to attempt the deadly Ladye Bay swim in Clevedon in the 19th century.

Sadly, the war put paid to her hobby, and she never resumed it again afterwards due to bringing up a family. I owe my love of open water swimming to her as I still remember to this day the songs she used to sing to me about her swimming experiences. These songs painted a picture which stayed with me well into adulthood until I finally took the plunge a few years ago.

Most of these songs are lost in the mists of time, but one particular ditty has stayed with me until this day. I had forgotten most of the lyrics but, remarkably, I was lucky enough to recover a dusty old cassette dated 1935 when searching through some of my grandmother's belongings.

The song goes as follows.

Never must a dryrobe wear
Till Halloween is in the air
And never wear thine neoprene
Until Advent is on the scene

Thine bikini shan't get wet
She hasn't been invented yet
And skinny dipping thou shan't do
Enlightened times are far from you

Never leave thine litter strewn
Or bad tidings will fall on you
But filthy water we don't care
We swim in sewage, we're not scared

Never stress 'bout feeling down
Stiff upper lip or thou willst drown
We only dip post cleaning spree
Then home to cook our husband's tea

All thine cake shalt be homemade
That processed crap is year's away
And only sip thine warm mulled wine
When it is almost Christmas time

Our cold swims are so much fun
The water is for everyone
But wild swimming thou shall not say
We called it swimming in my day.

The origins of the song are unknown. Maybe my grandmother wrote it herself, but the use of really old-fashioned words like thine and thou, suggests it may be much older. Sadly, the song reveals depressing attitudes towards the role of women in society, to environmental concerns and mental health issues. Remember though that this song is very much a product of its time and think of it as a positive thing the way our attitude towards these issues have progressed since then. Overall, I think the song shows a sense of the camaraderie we all share when cold water swimming and, for that reason, I believe we should treasure this link with the past.

The discovery of this song inspired me to start writing my own poems about swimming and some of the colourful characters I have met on my swimming journey. Disappointed by some of the attitudes shown in my grandmother's song, I also wrote poems about the environment, misogyny (most poignantly in my epic tribute to Betty and Mildred which, arguably, forms the centrepiece of this book), and mental health. Many of these poems are included in this collection. I hope you enjoy reading them.

SUNRISE

PART ONE

THE AWAKENING

"Every man has his secret sorrows
which the world knows not;
and often times we call a man cold
when he is only sad."
Henry Wadsworth Longfellow

THE AWAKENING

I await the morning with baited breath
The blast of the radio, the sound of a car
The persistent motions of the daily grind
The silent anguish which I watch from afar
How I long for the boredom of the daily commute
Buses full of the downcast all glued to their phones
The fatuous influence of futile celebrity
Surrounded by hordes though they travel alone
The news of the wars and the pain that they bring
Scrolled through, ignored then continue carefree
The plastic bottles, the coffee cups
Bought brand new, used once and sent out to sea
The pay packet the only goal
Of the frivolous mob parading the street
Packed like sardines in pursuit of obscurity
Pass so many faces they will never meet
How I long to return to those halcyon days
Free from the darkness with the nightmares dispatched
A plundered mind is a mind free of pain
A web of banality with humanity detached.

I WISH I WERE A MERMAID

I wish I were a mermaid
Forever in the sea
A life of peace and solitude
My days spent worry free
No need to stress 'bout trivia
No time for harsh regret
Untroubled in the water
The chance to soon forget
Adversity and tragedy
Submerged I'm full of glee
So, here's to all the mermaids
Forever in the sea.

WE SWIM

We swim for salvation, we swim for our soul
We swim for the friendship, we swim to feel whole
We swim when it's raining, we swim in the snow
We swim in all weathers, wherever we go
We swim in the rivers, the lakes and the sea
We swim where we can, we swim to be free
We swim for adventure, we bounce with the waves
We jump from the rocks and we're pulled through the caves
We swim to raise spirits, we swim for release
We swim without judgement, we swim to find peace
We swim to remember, we swim to get by
We swim so we live, we will swim till we die.

INVISIBLE

How good to be invisible
How great to disappear
Prepared to face the world each day
Escaping those I fear
Unleashed when I'm invisible
When no one knows my name
Where nobody knows who I am
Redeemed and free from shame
I wish the ground would open up
And swallow me up whole
A sanctuary away from here
Away from their control
I wish I were invisible
My frailties would mend
The judgement gone, at peace at last
Then all of this will end.

THE INTROVERT

Lost in my thoughts, I'm at one in my mind
Your comments affect me, so I hope you'll be kind
My dreams my salvation as I look back on life
Alone time my party time, where I'm safe from life's strife
Entrapped by the crowds, the noise is too much
I am not in their world, I am lost, out of touch
They intrude on my sanctum, oh please go away
But politeness my weakness, I allow them to stay
When I'm tired and I'm anxious and subdued by my mood
When I'm worn out, exhausted, I don't mean to sound
rude
But I need to escape, hide away and reflect
When I'm given this space, I've the chance to connect
There are times when I'd rather be left on my own
Know, your friendship I treasure; but I need time alone
I just want to feel loved, in my own happy place
Then I'll thrive on the freedom of the life I embrace.

IN MY DREAM

In my dream, you held me tight
Then smiled at me, I felt so sure
You held me through that long, cold night
With you beside me, I felt secure
In my dream, my dreams came true
We lay down there, you wanted me
I felt such warmth, you felt it too
Together now, we're meant to be
In my dream, we start again
We find the place where dreams are born
Where fantasy exists but when
The sun arrives, it's time to mourn
In my dream, brought under your spell
The sun shone brightly but I saw no light
I watched you leave and I bade you farewell
Then I woke in the morning, and returned to the night.

THE MERMAID

She dances to the tune of the ocean
Embracing all the magic of the sea
She celebrates the beauty of the water
She teaches us to be what we can be
Preparing for her latest crazy challenge
She's facing all the pain which drives her on
The water resonates deep in her spirit
She's cleansed when she's submerged, her demons gone
The children starstruck watching from the shoreline
They marvel at the mermaid flying past
Delight and wonder fill their happy faces
She's just as they imagined, oh so fast!
Ashore she has to face the shakes and shivers
With frozen feet she loses all her might
So elegant she seems within the water
On land she's lost but won't give up the fight
She's out to save the world, make sure you listen
And in return she'll give you a great show
She glides so smoothly as she surfs across the waves
Then swims into the distance, watch her go.

HER WORLD

Was this how things were meant to be?
Another day spent on the run
No means to heal the hurt inside
No place to flee, she'll never learn
She can't explain the isolation
Weighed down by feelings she'll never face
A cartoon exterior tries to impress
A brief flirtation with a loveless race
They soon move on, they soon forget
But still, she portrays a hopeful defiance
A million followers, few of them friends
Clings on for dear life, she's chained to her silence
Denied of their love, the gulf can't be filled
The mistrust and jealousy never ending
A thousand obstacles stand in her way
Her cry for help futile, the peril impending
Maybe tomorrow she'll start again
Abandon the leeches exploiting her purity
But once she's conceded she's tied to her fate
Afraid of escape, interred in obscurity.

VANITY

Consumed by her own vanity
Absorbed in her own world
She's shrouded in profanity
Her hubris is unfurled
Obsessed with her inanity
Where emptiness pervades
Detached from her humanity
Lost in pointless charades

Her vanity lacks parity
Vindictive in her views
Her mind full of vulgarity
Her sense of worth renews
She rules through her barbarity
In her empty domain
She'll never find her clarity
She can't explain her pain

The vanity, inanity
Profanity ignored
Disparity, no clarity
She falls upon her sword
A hostage to humanity
Defeated by conceit
Insanity breeds vanity
Her victimhood complete.

THE SWIMMER

Oblivious to the watching world
Chasing her demons to a desolate place
Before the tide turns, this is her race
The challenge she will always face
A danger she'll forever embrace
When she knows she's failed it's far too late
A mind befuddled, bewildered at sea
No time to retreat, no chance to flee
She carries on, what decides her fate?

WORLD'S END

The music still playing, singing sweet lullabies
To wish all a goodnight as the world around dies
The grasslands are scorched, not much there remains
A vast, unfilled wasteland of once mighty plains
The skies above empty, the bird song no more
Defined by a silence which chills to the core
The rain forests flattened, in a world of decay
Once a rainbow of colour, now a gravestone of grey
The flowers they wilt where the rain will not fall
In a drought-riven landscape which should terrify all
The rivers run dry, through the valleys of grief
Should we give up the ghost, should we lay nature's
wreath?
The winds of change howl, it is far too late now
The party is over, we destroyed this, somehow
A familiar face warns me, get ready my friend
I cannot be your Saviour. go, prepare for the end.

TIME TO SAY GOODBYE

When you know something's wrong
There's a hole in your heart
All you wanted is broken
And you need a fresh start
When it's time to move on
But you want to resist
Is it time to say goodbye?

The pleasure was mine
I promise you, but
Throughout your intrusion
I kept my mouth shut
Now you've made your decision
I'm sure I'll be fine
Is it time to say goodbye?

The look in your eyes
Was it real? was it fake?
There's no need for confusion
There's no need for debate
The path has been closed
Causing so much regret
Is it time to say goodbye?

The smiles and the laughs
And the close bond we made
Only caused disillusion
In time they should fade
But the hurt which it caused
Will stay deep in my bones
Is it time to say goodbye?

The joy in our minds
Seemed so real at the time
But the come down too strong
I could not face the climb
I felt chained to your aura

Which I could not escape
Is it time to say goodbye?

In the distance you'll fade
Then so soon you'll be gone
The mistakes I'll repeat
But at least I live on
In my heart all I know
There is nothing to gain
Is it time to say goodbye?

What's to come in the future?
Will I still know your name?
Will I ever concede
Who was really to blame?
That I just wasn't worthy
Of a place in your heart
It was time to say goodbye

Then when the time comes
When we're deep in the ground
None of these things will matter
To those still around
In the empty black hole
Of the life we once lived
Was I right to say goodbye?

WHAT I'VE BECOME

The river runs dry as it reaches the sea
Distance and time will not redefine
The crystal-clear springs where life once began
Which led me to this, to a fatal decline
A meandering stream once showed me the way
Till it merged with the ocean, I soon lost control
Blown around in the waves and thrown on to the rocks
No regret, no repentance for the lifetime you stole
A sanctified place where your purgatory reigns
Waiting in limbo for judgement to pass
No intervention can prevent what's to come
As the ghosts of my past surround me en-masse
Well-meant interference which once had me fooled
A cold, feigned indifference left me down on the floor
But why? And for what? Look at where we are now
In a twilight imprisoned, where you showed me the door
Descend to the seabed where shipwrecks lie still
Blood red is the sea where so many lie lost
No excuses are made, here we find no escape
In this sea of self-pity where we all pay the cost
Drown in the debris which engulfs me today
A drought of ideas suffocates what remains
But I won't reconsider, the decision is made
Overwhelmed by delusions which seep through my veins
Acceptance is all I wanted from you
Instead, a rebuttal, a refusal to act
A bleak and cruel future n this hollow recess
Your final demands leave me tied to your pact
The tide has gone out and it won't come back in
These the darkest of depths, I've been able to plumb
When all around see I am losing the fight
As I sit in my stupor, look at what I've become.

PART TWO

NO FUTURE

"The darkness is at its deepest.
Just before the sunrise."

Voltaire

SPRING

Too soon the spring it comes along
The birds engaged in vibrant song
The peaceful scene evades our mood
A chill still blows, the hope subdued
A forced reunion blisters the skin
The laughter fades, let sorrow begin
The days grow longer, feeling inside
Gung-ho with anguish intensified
And when we wither and fall apart
The sun which shines will break our heart
With caution borne on a slippery slope
These new beginnings, they bring false hope
The nights too short, the days too warm
We curse this never-ending storm
Confusion reigns, our heads in a spin
Awakened emotions, deceive us within.

NO FUTURE

Today there's no future
At least not for me
No sense of belonging
No way to be free
The depths I have sunk to
Escape not a choice
Entrapped by bad judgement
Condemned with no voice
No path to redemption
No route to the stars
My road to Hell final
Defined by these scars
All hope is a smokescreen
Resigned to my fate
All love has been vanquished
Abandoned for hate
My story is over
No strength to go on
Constrained by this bedlam
Too soon I'll be gone
Maybe I'll be happy
When I'm safe from this fear
When this torture is over
When I'm no longer here.

ALONE

Alone in the evening
Alone in the night
Alone in the morning
Alone in this fight
Alone when I'm lonely
Alone in a crowd
Alone when I'm silent
Alone when I'm loud
Alone when I'm happy
Alone when I'm sad
Alone when I'm laughing
Alone when I'm mad
Alone in my nightmares
Alone in my dreams
Alone when I'm struggling
Alone with my screams
Alone since my childhood
Alone every day
Alone when I'm with you
Alone when I pray
Alone when embarrassed
Alone when ashamed
Alone when I'm broken
Alone when untamed
Alone when I'm anxious
Alone when with friends
Alone with my demons
Alone till life ends.
Alone in my future
Alone in my past
Alone in my darkness
Alone to the last.

CHILDHOOD

Alone in the night- the one place I'm safe
The tears free to flow- known only to me
The morning brings dread- the fear of the call
The call to arise- to face the cruel world
Too anxious outside- please don't make me go
The school is my hell- still haunts me today
Afraid of my peers- I hide in my shell
No friends and no hope- I'm locked there in fear
The lessons unclear- my mind just a blur
Don't want to be here- I pray for the bell
The time moves so slow - the bell rung too late
No sanctuary at home- no chance to escape
Afraid to go out- avoiding them all
No place in their world- no prospect of peace
Forever I'm lost- still tied to those days
Alone in the night- I pray for release.

A DIFFERENT WORLD

In the corner where we once hid
The cobwebs advancing through years of neglect
Adventures embraced when young and naive
The peril faced daily, devoid of regret.
The culture changed, our screens now King
They glisten in colour, not black and white
A wind encircles, decreases our reach
Our lives depicted in virtual flight
A different world from the one we knew
But the conflicts and fall outs the same as before
So little has changed from days gone by
Just different players in a different war.

CADENCE OF LIFE

Obliquely fashioned into a predatory state
Penetrating boundaries and teasing conclusions
Generosity evolves to an illusionary spate
Of rabid hunters probing their affusions
Disbelieving the one he must trust
An affliction since childhood demanding reprisal
Tarnished and punished to where needs must
The things deemed essential to his survival
Expression forbidden in the womb of his hellion
A minion of virtue exposed to distress
Eager to please but prone to rebellion
His mind interrupted, a calamitous mess
Preened to perfection, refusing advice
That forces rejection, the cadence of life.

VIEW FROM THE PIER

Clouds on the horizon, but they don't threaten me
The autumn light bright with the sun roaming free
She glistens so clearly, on the water below
We cling to the sunshine; we don't want to let go
But, as sunset arrives, we know winter is near
With the clouds closing in, Nature's message is clear
Once emblazoned with colour, now darkness pervades
With reckless abandon, all hope and joy fades
A chilling wind haunts us as night takes control
A harsh, ghostly presence which will swallow us whole
Then a foreboding current, leaves us out in the cold
Our time was too short, now death reaps a grim hold
All we're left with is memories but, they too, will be gone
With the end closing in, there's no chance to move on
All the times we felt happy, all those times we ran wild
But here, time waits for no man, no woman or child.

AUTUMN MORNING

The mist will not lift on this late autumn day
And the damp, chilling air, will not blow away
The trees they stand naked with nothing to show
Whilst their berries lie rotting, on the ground down below
An eerie, spooked silence fills the air in this place
The birdsong long gone, this a dreary, dank space
The days ever shorter, the nights never end
When we share in this sorrow, there's no need to pretend
Each day left to scavenge like wild dogs and rats
Much better to hibernate like the hedgehogs and bats
When purgatory lingers far too long on the heart
No signs of new life, all our dreams fall apart
Please hurry on winter, bring crisp sunny days
So, we're freed from the gloom of this autumnal haze
With no flowers, no colour, no beauty in sight
We will wait for the snowdrops, the return of the light.

ANY QUESTIONS?

Any questions to ask me before I go?
It's the last chance saloon, it's the end of the show
Any stories or secrets, you would like me to share?
When I go, they'll leave with me, but who knows, to where?
Any times I upset you or my taunts made you weep
I will ask your forgiveness before I go to sleep
Any feelings you need to declare then please do
But don't say you love me as I know that's not true
We all make mistakes and I've made plenty here
As I'm fading away, let me make myself clear
That I tried all I could to be good, though I failed
That I self-destructed, then my demons prevailed
So much I regret, now we've run out of time
We're apart, not together, what a waste, what a crime
Now none of this matters, all the tears were in vain
We had chances but blew it, you won't see me again
Any anger, resentment, then please let it go
My time is now over but yours isn't so know
When my ashes are scattered in the wind, I'll run free
Then you'll have a fresh start in a world without me.

PLEASE DON'T MOURN FOR ME

Please don't mourn for me
Tomorrow I'll be gone
The loneliness incurable
The world will soon move on

Please don't mourn for me
At last, I'm free of pain
The times I cried in agony
Those days won't come again

Please don't mourn for me
I'm finally at peace
Escape evaded me in life
But now I have release

Please don't mourn for me
Today I lost the fight
The sunset though was beautiful
Remember me tonight.

FALLING UNDER

Shines in me
Whilst I'm sleeping
In the daylight
Disappears
Climbing over
Falling under
Distant ages
Far away

Me to you
Lost in time
Days remembered
By us all
Taking over
Falling under
In the mist
Kept apart

Not aroused
Not dependent
All around us
Pleased as punch
Never over
Falling under
Out of reach
Out of touch

Future forecast
Not in favour
Not my vision
Your abuse
Vacant skylines
Falling under
Act out nightmares
No excuse.

THROUGH DEPRESSION

This wasn't the life I'd been hoping for
When I was young with my feet on the ground
Is this all delusion or is it all real?
Fatigue rules today but tomorrow I'll bound
My energy full as I smile through the day
Deep down there's a cry heard only by me
The view on the outside says all is well
But writing this poem will not set me free

The low mood pervades, swathes of sadness surround
Feeling helpless and hopeless, low esteem grinds me
down
Indecisive and anxious, motivation is gone
No pleasure is gained, all denied till I drown
In a sea full of grief, fuelled by waves of false guilt
Locked away from the world, in self-pity I hide
Irritated, not eating, I am losing control
Am I ill or just lazy or just too bleary eyed?

The tears won't stop flowing, I am under their spell
My fear of outside means I can't face much more
In the crowds all is empty, there I feel so alone
Due to overexposure, I am frightened and sore
Through the depths of despair is it time to give in?
As I exit my body, I emerge way up high
In a moment of sense, I reach out for some help
But I'm told I won't find it and I won't be told why

On the edge of the cliff, I look out to the sea
Then the view which goes down to the beach where I'll
fall
With no future to plan for, seems the easy way out
I hate to give in, but I've given my all
But the fall seems too final, I cannot face the end
In my mind I see beauty in the ocean below
Something I can cling on to, just a glimmer of hope
In my heart I'm confounded, Should I stay? Should I go?

The light which I'd hoped for, seems so far, there I'll head
Ignoring the danger, all the time in a daze
Where it leads, I can't tell, where I've been I don't know
An oasis of calm when I'm freed from your gaze
In the water I'll go, to my one, true escape
There I swim and I swim until I feel I'm sure
That I'm safe from all harm, from your cruel, spiteful reign
Then released from your prison and the pain is no more.

DEPARTURE LOUNGE

Anxiety builds as I wait for your call
My time not yours to give away
But your decisions define me still
The wait for you absorbs my day
I stand in fear of the road ahead
A path unwanted, it must not prevail
Determination not sustained
The final straw, resigned to fail
A final push to banish my past
A chance not taken, the end in sight
Into the departure lounge I go
Unsure of my fate, I face the night.

PART THREE

HOPE

"Rest but never quit.
Even the sun has a sinking spell each evening.
But it always rises the next morning.
At sunrise, every soul is born again."
Muhammad Ali

HOPE

Through the darkest of hours there is always hope
Through the bleakest of nights, I shall not give in
When my path is blocked, and the road ahead closed
When the cloud filled skies mean I cannot win
But the clouds will pass, and the mist will clear
Then the sun will rise in the morning sky
From our lowest mood there's a way ahead
To a happy ending which could be nearby
For our sweetest moments, they are yet to come
We will find belief with our faith restored
We shall make a promise, form a bond in trust
With the outlook good, life can be adored
Things are bleak for now, but it cannot last
When the wind is strong, pain is blown away
Happiness will find us, but it won't be rushed
Then, with patience, we will find a better day.

THE LAKE

I know that she'll be waiting
When I need her, she'll be there
She glistens with the sunrise
Swathes of mist soon fill her air
They arrive and soon I follow
With their friendship, I'll survive
Through my struggles. they're beside me
My inner mermaid keeps me alive.

I know all of the faces
The names learnt through the years
Their candour and their openness
The loneliness, the tears
Her depths no friend of suffering
Forgotten for today
The reason why we swim here
She keeps our pain at bay

Her welcome cruel, this morning
In the brutal Arctic wind
No mercy as we enter
But the screams, they soon rescind
Plunge in in solidarity
The adversity brings us strength
Serenity rules, baptised with new life
Keeps our demons at arms length

Whether ice miler or dipper
Or Gav stood on the side
"I've been in already"
His mantra cried with pride
The diversity of the characters
The warming wintry embrace
The water a friend but the people my saviours
Purged and cleansed, my happy place.

IN THEIR FOOTSTEPS

A post swim stroll around Poets Walk.

Where frozen feet
Reach muddy peaks
Our canine friends sense freedom
Up and down
We're warming now
An inner peace emerges
We skirt around
The hallowed ground
The child entombed, at peace now
The pungent glades
Where Billy wades
The boats rest far from sea here
Up we go
The view below
Hope framed beyond the mudflats
Where poets walked
A peace they sought
Their stamping ground augments us
So down we go
The pier on show
She radiates, resplendent
Down to the shore
Our faith restored
The lake appears, at home now
The view below
The place we go
Where friends all meet
The place we know.

REFLECTIONS

So lonely, so still
Forever in stone
No plaque to remember
Just lies there alone
We visit her often
To rest, take a breath
Perspectives regained
On life and on death
We treasure the friendship
We've found in this place
On these cold winter mornings
There's a warmth we embrace
Our walk will continue
But the memories won't end
Reflect in the moment
Rest easy my friend.

THE PIER

No fun to be had, no amusements or fayre
No smell of stale junk food left filling the air
No crash of the dodgems, no wall of loud noise
No cheap tacky shops selling cheap tacky toys
No rugby or football shown on giant screens
No theatre shows starring faded has-beens
No hot dogs or doughnuts or candy floss here
No need for such features on old Clevedon pier
A place to recharge and to rest far from shore
Remembering loved ones who stood here before
Immersed in the view of the sea from up high
Reflect and unwind as the world passes by.

THE WATERFALL

The birdsong disrupting our silent retreat
Across tranquil meadows we amble ahead
Refreshed by the storm, the waters replete
In vision her beauty raises the dead
In awe of her power, we ponder a while
Remain at a distance till patience has strayed
A wade in the stream indulges a smile
Inspired by the romance, new memories made
Bewitched by her charm, by the bite of the cold
We're taken aback by the force of her roar
Submerged in the waters, the magic takes hold
Ensconced in the scene, we leave wanting more
We depart, full of joy, in the spell of her breeze
Here, the sun never breaches the shade of the trees.

TO PUBLOW

All Saints standing tall, surveying the scene
A village at peace, a place lost in time
The fields all around, so mellow, so green
A new day begins, she's seen in her prime
With Acker on watch, his words ring so true
So little has changed, the children still play
In shallows below, in waters he knew
Enthralled by her charm, we're tempted today
From Chew Lake she came, to Keynsham she'll go
The river runs through, the birds full of song
Alone in her depths, untouched by the flow
So still at first light, the peace won't last long
The wagtails at play, they dance to her tune
The strangers on shore appear way too soon.

MUCHELNEY

The bridge forms a shadow on the river below
In clear waters the reeds and the fish stem the flow
The blazing hot sun sometimes there, sometimes not
Though the clouds won't deter us from this beautiful spot
The scene so serene cannot last in this place
The boats and the paddleboards take up much of our
space
Whilst walkers and cyclists pass us chatting away
Both the sun and the silence intermittent today
Will we brave the cool waters? Plunge below with the
fish?
As we jump from the pontoon with eyes closed, we both
wish
For this dream to continue, to forget the bad days
Swimble downstream for Langport, in the autumnal haze
The current is weak, and the reed beds grow wide
As you're stifled and struggling, I will not leave your side
Turn around back to safety, to the pontoon we head
As the reeds start to thin, calm replaces our dread
Here we're frozen in time as the world passes by
Where a buzzard and swallows fill the late summer sky
We emerge from the water where we dry in the sun
In the sporadic silence we're at peace, we're as one
Till the cloud kills the moment, it is time to move on
We'll return here in winter, when the crowds are long
gone.

SUMMER REGRET

The sun beating down, the sweat fills my brow
Feeling drowsy and listless, bemused, out of touch
My focus distracted, soon lost in the haze
How we wish to escape, this torture so much
For months we've been praying for these warm days to
come
We dreamt through the winter, mourned as spring stalled
too long
All the rain and the wind, all the cloud and cool air
Led to what we now have, like a furnace, burns strong
As we try but we fail to cool down we lambast
Our love of the summer, turns to dust every time
We roast in her swelter, we long for some shelter
But to waste on God's gift would be too big a crime
So, we soak up the sun, make the most of the day
Growing faint in her heat, dehydrate in her glow
As the forests ignite, as the fields scorch and die
Let this come to an end, but we know, yes, we know
That when autumn returns, that when winter takes hold
With the cold biting wind, all too soon we'll forget
Then we'll ache for the summer and the long sultry days
Our eternal lament lost in summer regret.

FIRST SWIM OF AUTUMN

A solitary apple clinging on for dear life
When it drops in the water, nature's bounty is gone
The first frost of winter is closing in fast
With the nights getting colder as summer moves on
We head for the river in the cold morning air
Leave the city behind as we start a new day
Sunday morning at sunrise with the world still asleep
Where the threat of the cold will not keep us away
The morning mist clearing as we walk on ahead
The trees which surround, stand so tall and so proud
Cast a dark and bleak shadow on the water below
Though the view brings a peace, leaves us calm and
unbowed
We ready ourselves in the biting cold wind
Then we enter with screams of despair and dismay
Once submerged though, we're freed, peace of mind
takes control
With the silence surrounding, as we swimble away
The sun battles hard to rise clear of the trees
So, we float on downstream where her light breaches
through
Meditate in her glory, in reflection and praise
This a time to be thankful, to revive and renew
We seem frozen in time as we bathe in her rays
But the cold won't forgive us if we linger too long
Here the last of the blackberries fill the bank to our side
Like the summer they'll pass but our spirit stays strong
Emerge from the water, let the shivers begin
Where our icy core brings a warm glow to our heart
Relieved from the stresses of everyday life
We're refreshed and alive, we can sense a new start
Deep down we all know that when winter takes hold
When frost carpets the fields, when thick fog fills the air
We'll embrace winter's wonder, energised by her force
Taking joy from our suffering, in our cold water prayer.

EMPTY SPACE

Below in the darkness is an empty space
Which will never be filled, which I'll never resolve
Drawn into the void by a restless state
My passion reined in as temptations evolve
An empty resonance sates a strange desire
For this broken mind scarred by toxic finds
Where an empty childhood borne of cloud filled skies
Led to years of sorrow shaped by childlike minds
Where a barren vista leaves me cursed and lost
Forged by empty visions, drawn in unkempt joy
Still immersed in sadness in this empty place
In this grief filled world which I can't enjoy
Then a sense of wonder sees my faith restored
Sailing tranquil oceans so serene and calm
Where my soul is soothed, and my mind renewed
In the empty space I feel safe from harm.

WHEN

When will I know it is time to accept
That I am who I am, take the time to reflect
On mistakes I have made, on the flawed path I chose
Where I froze out of fear, when those choices arose.

When will I learn that night follows day
That the simple things matter, I can find my own way
To be true to myself and not drawn to your lore
Should I stray in the water when I'm safe on the shore?

When will I find that I just cannot be
Like you or like anyone, other than me
That my life is my own, and perhaps I'll be fine
If I make good decisions, there is still time to shine.

When will I find my own path in a place
Where jealousy rules, where I can't keep the pace
To forget and forgive, take the chance to be me
As I dance to my own tune, let me be what I'll be.

When will I see that the troubles I face
Cannot be defeated, that I won't win this race
By embracing these limits, there's a chance to move on
And accept when my dreams are all dead and all gone.

When will I choose to emerge from the dark
When the light draws me out it is time to embark
On the road facing forward, turn my back on the past
Face the sun as it's rising, then the sadness won't last.

When will I learn not to aim for the stars
That it's fine just to aim for the moon or for Mars
Some will aim far too high, they will never arrive
With my aims more simplistic, there's a chance I could thrive.

When the end comes, will I still feel the same
Will it all have been worth it, will the world know my name?
Or will I be forgotten like so many before
Life is cruel, life is short, will I leave wanting more?

PART FOUR

SUNRISE

"We can only appreciate the miracle of a sunrise
if we have waited in the darkness."

Sapna Reddy

EVERLASTING LIFE

Liam says we'll live forever
And I hope that he is right
No one really wants to die
Keep the day and lose the night
Immortality means chances
Won't be wasted, nothing spurned
We can do whatever pleases
Safe from harm, no lessons learned
Relax, chill out, no need to rush
There's always another day
The options are unlimited
An eternity to play.

The life which lasts forever
The idea it makes me weep
My world's a shitshow as it is
Endless life? I'd rather sleep
And because we don't live forever
We should treasure every day
The experience more valuable
When you've watched time ebb away
Thank goodness we're not immortal
Thank goodness Liam's wrong
Live every day as if your last
Well, it's such a silly song.

THE BUTTERFLY

The Butterflies flitter and flutter away
Flapping their wings over fields full of flowers
Wasting my day as I watch them at play
Alone in my thoughts as I squander the hours
The lavender meadows arouse my desire
Aromas entice with the backdrop serene
The skylarks above, rising higher and higher
Their ascent one of wonder, their view filled with green
I hope soon to share in the butterfly's lair
To dance in the yarrow and aster so free
Unhindered by sorrow, to flirt without care
My troubles forgotten, at last, I can see
But the butterfly mortal, disappears way too soon
As the summer flowers wilt, we are losing the light
In the darkness I'm blinded by the glare of the moon
Like the butterfly's spirit, I shall fade in the night.

FOREVER GONE

Observe their gravestones
So many stories
Ones never heard
Or told again
The years of struggle
Of lives so frugal
The facts on record
Their tales unknown
Their darkest hours
Their pride and glory
All lost forever
Forever gone.

All those who knew them
Now lie beside them
The rest eternal
Perpetual cold
The peace is shattered
By revelations
That soon we'll join them
Our plight recalled
Entombed beside them
Our lives forgotten
Explore the chasm
Forever gone

The birds still singing
The grass keeps growing
The world continues
As it's always done
But through the ages
We turn the pages
Things ever changing
Our fate is known
Our pleasure short lived
Love and forgiveness
Lost in the thick mist

Forever gone

The world around us
Will soon surround us
But still, she's mortal
In time will end
Our days are numbered
Our faith encumbered
The storm will take us
Another time
Our lives redundant
Soon on the gravestones
Our names in writing
Forever gone.

BALLOONS

Early morning
Waiting and hoping
The first time we see them
Excitement builds

Soon they fly over
Wait for the explosion
We count as they pass
One after another

The sky is now full
All shapes and all sizes
A rainbow of colour
Delight on our faces

Some fly so high
Some come so low
We wave as they pass
Then watch them grow smaller

They fade in the distance
Just a few stragglers now
So soon they are gone
Skies empty above us.

DO YOU KNOW

Do you know
How wonderful you are
How you get me through the pain
How you make my heart sing
Do you know
How I'm spellbound by your smile
When you look into my eyes
When you make me feel alive
Do you know
That I miss you more each day
That I long to hold you tight
Through the long and lonely nights
Do you know
How I treasure every moment
Of our magical adventures
Of the beauty you display
Do you know
How I long to see you now
How I'm lost when you're not here
In my daydreams all the time
And do you know
I will never leave your side
When the darkness spreads around you
In your moments of self-doubt
I hope you know
That I feel this love for you
That I hope to be beside you
That I hope you feel it too.

HAPPINESS

To find a friend who understands
To find new places where we can play
To feel the sun's warmth on our skin
To share in adventure on a cloudless day

To lie back and listen to the sound of the waves
As they crash down below, hear the song of the sea
To swim and explore in secret, dark caves
To jump from the rocks so naked and free

To lose inhibition, feeling safe and secure
To sip on fresh coffee as we share in the view
To escape all the sadness which brought us both here
To rest side by side, I'm at peace when with you

To let the warm breeze dry us off as we snooze
Feeling safe and content with no thoughts of regret
But this window of happiness gone way too soon
In this moment of time, I shall never forget.

VIEW FROM THE BENCH

I'm at peace with the world, when admiring this view
Of the valley below, where I swam, when with you
The lost sounds of summer, so silent today
Though the memories linger, when I let my mind stray
That brief moment in time, when our lives were as one
Too soon it was over, but, at least, we had fun
That late summer evening as we watched the sun set
The sound as the gate crashed, one we'll never forget
The memories special but those feelings, now gone
That evening escaped us but, in life, we move on
We were lost in the mist, but the mist is now clear
And the view below perfect, and I know you're still near
I'm revived in your presence and I feel I'm reborn
As the calmness engulfs me on this warm winter morn
Then at last, I move on, I accept and I grow
This, my view from the bench of the valley below.

I'LL BE THERE

I'll be there when you're feeling alone
When you're losing your mind
When you've lost all you've known
I'll be there when you're deep in a hole
When you feel overwhelmed
When you're out of control
I'll be there when you're troubled by grief
When faith deserts you
When you've no self-belief
I'll be there when you're feeling betrayed
When you're haunted by nightmares
When you're cold and afraid
I'll be there when your strength is all gone
When you're down in the doldrums
When you can't carry on
I'll be there when your future looks bleak
When you feel like a failure
When your mind's lame and weak
I'll be there when talking's too tough
When you long for some silence
When enough is enough
I'll be there on your judgement day
When the world is against you
When you've been led astray
I'll be there when you need a friend
When you're feeling abandoned
When the night will not end
I will be there, and when I need you
When I'm struggling, I know
You'll be there for me too.

IN THE WAVES

In the waves, the waves of life
Thrown up and down, then blown around
When in the waves, where friendships form
We face the storm, where waves abound
In the waves, we live to swim
We face the danger, we face our fear
Trust and acceptance, when in the waves
Our love of water, where love is near
In the waves, stick side-by-side
We float serenely, our bond will grow
Reprieved together, we swim as one
Through bleak, cold days, through rain and snow
In the waves, from Ladye Bay
Swept past the hotel, then through the pier
We reach the beach, we scramble out
The swim complete, our thoughts now clear
In the waves, we break the spell
We smile throughout these special days
The celebrations, with friends met here
We toast the water, then sing her praise
In the waves, we soon forget
Our troubles fading, the light will come
The friendly banter, the jokes we share
Down on the pebbles, we won't succumb
To winter's cold, when in the waves
We'll win this battle, soon snug and warm
Hot chocolate shared, with squirty cream
Our comfort earned, safe from the storm
The sunset savoured, lost in the waves
Accept, move on, what's done is done
Purged in the ocean, the waves we faced
Reborn together, in the waves as one.

TO BE HAPPY

To be happy and to savour all the good times when they come
To have hope when things aren't looking great, when you're feeling kind of glum
To battle on when times are hard, in the hope life will improve
And to not down tools or lose your faith when life doesn't hit the groove
To smile and keep on smiling when, perhaps, you don't know why
But to know life isn't perfect, and at times, it's fine to cry
To not feel shamed or troubled, by your failings and mistakes
But acknowledge it when things go wrong, when you just can't get the breaks
To look forward to the future but to not hide from your past
To aim to be the best you can, but no shame to finish last
To feel safe from any danger, to steer clear from any harm
But still take a chance and take a risk with no need to feel alarm
To be honest, always love yourself, make the most of every day
But to still relax, to take time out, to ponder on your way
To share your finest moments, when you feel you can't do wrong
But to not show off or act too proud, neither celebrate too long
To know life isn't easy, there will be hard times ahead
But to make the most of what you have, not be overcome by dread
To have everything you'll ever want and all you'll ever need
But to still own next to nothing, and to not be ruled by greed

To love your friends and say well done, whenever they do
well
And to not be bound by jealousy, never let your envy
dwell
To be grateful for their kindness when they give their best
to you
Then pay them back with interest, be the best friend, keep
things true
To feel lucky, know your blessings, when good fortunes
on your side
But to not appear too bitter, when life's pleasures are
denied
To encourage good in others, whether they be friend or
foe
But to not demand perfection, that is not the way to go
To accept there will be days and weeks where things
don't look so bright
But to always stick together, maybe then, we'll be alright
To have self-belief, to not give up, give yourself the time
to shine
To be thankful, to be happy, when the stars, at last, align.

SUNRISE

Out of the darkness shines a glimmer of light
When I'm down on my knees I won't give up the fight
When I'm faced with uncertainty, and I'm plagued by
mistrust
When I drown in my tears and it's hard to adjust
To the rhythm of life and the turmoil inside
Through the grief and bereavement where a part of me
died
When I can't face the world or the people I meet
When anxiety builds and I freeze with cold feet
When I fear for my future with what lies ahead
When I'd rather stay home and stay safe in my bed
When the rainstorms outside match the tone of my mood
When I've reached my nadir, is it time to conclude
That from my lowest ebb, I can only ascend
That the darkest of tunnels will eventually end
That the floods will subside, wash the sadness away
That the fires will burn out, then we'll see a new day
When the tides on my side and the current has turned
When the future looks bright, given all I have learned
I will bathe in the beauty where an inner peace lies
In the light of the sunrise, when I open my eyes.

RAINBOW

The gloom is clearing, a rainbow in sight
Swathes of bright colour meet the morning air
Freed from the chains of dark clouds in the night
Blinded by light and the strength of her glare
Once there was thunder and rain, now there's bliss
Views full of wonder, not landscapes of grey
New life takes over, freed from the abyss
A sense of belief has found us today
A pot of gold waits for those who believe
Magical unicorns reach for the stars
The sun our saviour, we gain our reprieve
Beauty surrounds us then softens our scars
Rainbows of colourful joy fill the sky
Black clouds chased away; we wave them goodbye.

SUNSET

These poems did not fit in
with the general theme of Sunrise,
but I thought they were worth sharing.

BETTY AND MILDRED

Many regular Clevedon swimmers have completed the famous Ladye Bay to Pier swim. What a lot of people don't know is that the Ladye Bay swim has a fascinating history going back to Victorian times.

Clevedon began to gain popularity as a coastal resort with the opening of the Clevedon branch line in 1847. Thousands would visit Clevedon to take in the sights and sounds, including the now famous pier which was built in the 1860s. Sea bathing became popular during this time, and many swam off the main beach by the pier. Sadly, women were excluded from participating as it was considered highly inappropriate for women and men to swim together at this time.

In 1873, the decision was taken to open a new beach at North Clevedon Bay. The beach was considered ideal for women only bathing due to its secluded and sheltered location. The beach was renamed Ladies Bay and soon women were able to enjoy the health benefits of open water swimming. In order to protect the safety of the women swimming at the beach, a viewing platform was built to the south of the beach so that responsible males could keep an eye on the swimmers. However, it was not long before this became a popular venue for moustached Victorian men with binoculars to take the opportunity to perv on the women in the hope of catching the occasional glimpse of an ankle. This viewing platform is still there today and is well worth a visit for those interested in local history.

In the late 19th century, the suffragette movement was becoming increasingly popular, and many women were feeling unhappy that they were excluded from swimming by the pier. A plan was hatched by two brave women, Mildred Summerhayes and Betty Wright. They would swim down from Ladye Bay and exit the water on their arrival at the pier beach. Sadly, Betty drowned somewhere by the hotel, but Mildred made it all the way to the beach. Her arrival caused a right commotion as you can probably imagine. Mildred though, was unperturbed and calmly exited the water before embarking on the walk back to Ladye Bay to collect her stuff. Sadly, she did not have room for her dryrobe and flask in her tow float and she passed away on her walk back to Ladye Bay due to hypothermia.

These two heroes were not forgotten though and many women were inspired to follow their example. There are over one hundred recorded examples of women completing this swim over the next ten years and no doubt there are countless others who we don't know about. Clevedon Town Council were eventually forced to bow to pressure and both beaches were opened up to one and all (apart from dogs on the Pier beach which are still banned to this day).

Over the following decades, the Ladye Bay swim became increasingly popular, almost exclusively with women. Many believe that Phillip Duma holds the record for the longest Ladye Bay swim with an impressive 14 ways in 2020 but the record is actually held by Gertrude Higginbottom who swam an incredible TWENTY-TWO ways in 1936. Sadly, the intervention of war in 1939 meant women had more important things to be getting on with and open water swimming ceased to be a major leisure activity until Wim Hof reintroduced it during lockdown.

So, there we have it. If you are inspired to do this swim, remember to be thankful to Betty and Mildred who made it possible all those years ago. Make sure to train properly beforehand though and always swim with a tow float, a whistle and a phone and never swim alone.

Inspired by this wonderful story, I composed this poem.

THE STORY OF BETTY AND MILDRED

A long time ago in the days of Queen Vic
The nation discovered the joys of the sea
The trains stretched to Clevedon with crowds thousands thick
To the beach they were heading, for the day they were free
A day free from work and the toil and the grind
For a stroll on the prom or a trip to the pier
Maybe lunch in the Salty, better chips you won't find
But this vision of heaven was not oh so clear

The hordes they gathered on the pebbles below
The men with moustaches, dressed smartly and proud
The Victorian man, he was always on show
A stiff upper lip, blending in with the crowd
Draconian dress codes, no chance to have fun
Their place in society depends on conformity
Their formal attire out of place in the sun
But no one complained, they observed uniformity

But where were the women, there were none on the beach
Their absence a mystery to our more modern minds
The days of bikinis were years out of reach
The women's mere presence forbidden on signs
'No women allowed' for they breed dirty thoughts
Send men out of hand with their urge and desire
The slovenly strumpets, much trouble they brought
Best keep them apart or be soiled in their mire

A mile to the north, all the ladies must go
To the new Ladye Bay, secluded and sure
Sheltered from currents and dangerous flow
Of the treacherous waters, keep them covered and pure
These weak, feeble creatures unsafe in the sea
A viewpoint was built, keeps them all safe from harm
In no time at all, men rushed there with glee

For a glance of an ankle or a glimpse of an arm

The women compliant, they had no choice
The men held the power, kept their wives in their place
But two of the ladies had a contrasting voice
Two rebellious harlots with no ladylike grace
Their ambition was strong, they'd swim under the pier
But their dreams and true life could never align
Turned away by the guards, left despondent, in tears
"It says no dogs allowed, can you not read the sign?"

Left red faced, embarrassed, the two ladies fled
On the way to their cars, in their shame, they soon ran
Facing jeers as the news of their failed attempt spread
Still fuming and angry at the bigoted ban
But Mildred and Betty, for those were their names
Remained unperturbed, they were not beaten yet
Clear in intention, succinct in their aims
They soon hatched a plan, but they'd need to get wet

The masterplan made, they'd embark on their tour
From Ladye Bay to be swept past the pier
So much could go wrong, but they both felt so sure
They'd swim in their birthday suits, soon they'd appear
To outrage and anger from lecherous men
The surprise guaranteed to reign chaos and bedlam
With the thrill of the swim, they would feel born again
Leave the men feeling dirty, depraved, vile and then some

So, the big day arrived but the weather not great
A storm in the sky but no thoughts they might quit
The plight of all women would hinge on their fate
They knew they could do more than clean, cook and knit
With no health and safety or phones to check tides
Braced ready for danger, they were soon on their way
Was sure to be a bouncy and hazardous ride
With fear and foreboding they swam from the bay

Their tow floats too small for their dryrobes and flasks

They were taking a risk with the storm at its peak
Both under prepared for this arduous task
They were taking on water, things were looking quite
bleak
Mildred felt strong but Betty would wane
By the Walton Hotel she would give up the fight
Engulfed by the waves, by the sea she was slain
On the seabed she lay, to be fish food that night

Mildred distraught but she wouldn't stop there
Persistent and dogged she swam on ahead
The pier in her sights, Betty deep in her prayers
With the waves all around she could sense only dread
But the current was strong, she was soon gaining speed
She flew under the pier, and she soon reached the shore
She clambered out safely, was finally freed
The men full of shock, their jaws dropped to the floor

The men bewildered by what they had seen
As bold as brass, Mildred acting the slut
To the men such actions so naughty, obscene
Forget arms and ankles they had seen boobs and butt
But Mildred not there for a sordid display
She was making a point about women's rights
Not one man had swum down from Ladye Bay
Yet a feeble, weak woman 'had now scaled those heights

No hanging about with police on their way
She walked to the bay to reclaim her stuff
But her dryrobe and hot drink seemed so far away
She was starting to shiver, still unclothed, in the buff
Getting weaker and weaker, Ladye Bay seemed too far
She lay down for a rest with tears in her eyes
Her struggle traumatic yet strangely bizarre
As she lay down, she knew she would ne'er again rise

Mildred was buried in an unmarked grave
An outcome too common in Victorian times
For the whores and the hussies who failed to behave

They would never reach heaven after such sleazy crimes
But Mildred lived on through the Ladye Bay swim
For thousands would follow, though many would fall
With the ban on mixed bathing considered too grim
Soon enough the beach opened to one and to all

So, remember these icons on your next Clevedon jaunt
They both gave their lives so that we could be free
From division and hatred and insults and taunts
In order to save us they were killed by the sea
Oh, Mildred and Betty, we honour your valiance
No longer are women the property of men
And thanks to your teasing, your cheek and your dalliance
We will all swim at Clevedon again and again.

A FEW MORE
SWIMMING POEMS

WINTER WARRIORS

Brave, brave Winter warriors
Swimming along the wall
No swimming out to the pontoon
That wouldn't be safe at all

Not one of them complaining
About the ice and cold
The friendly chatter after
They have such fun, I'm told

Not like me with my cold hands
Squealing all the time
The moment I plunge the icy depths
I whine and whine and whine

One day I hope I'm brave enough
To Warrior with Row
To swim and smile and celebrate
Off to the lake we go.

THREE SILLY FRIENDS

Three friends they turned up for a swim
Acting all hard and tough
They chose to ignore the safety signs
Oh well, that's fair enough

The first friend dived into the lake
And landed on his head
The medics tried to rescue him
But sadly, he was dead

Friend number two went for a run
Along the high sea wall
He slipped and broke his back below
Oh, what a nasty fall!

The third friend came straight from the pub
And jumped into the lake
He had a massive heart attack
And couldn't eat his cake

What can we learn from these three friends?
They sadly are no more
Always obey the safety signs
Or you might well be done for.

CAKE

Whenever we go for a swim at the lake
No trip is complete unless there is cake
Whether flapjacks or ginger or carrot, all's good
Lemon drizzle or chocolate, you know that you would
In the winter, cakes needed, when we're cold and we're wet
For the energy boost, for the comfort we get
When the shivers take hold, and we need something sweet
No swimmer would ever decline such a treat
But, always make sure that the cake is homemade
The shop bought stuff isn't the same I'm afraid
Cake brings us together, keeps our hunger at bay
So, get baking, I'm starving, and I want CAKE today.

BRAVE PHILLIP

I met a man called Phillip
We swam to Ladye Bay
So fast he flew right past me
He blew me right away

He tried to win the Long Swim
Oh my, the mind it boggles
But sadly for brave Phillip
He lost his hat and goggles

The swim across the channel
Promised a better day
But sadly for brave Phillip
He gave up at halfway

He swam to Ladye Bay and back
An amazing seven times
But sadly for brave Phillip
No medal, what a crime

At last, he won the Long Swim
To make his son go wow
But sadly for brave Phillip
His son preferred the cow

So off he went to Poland
Where the water was so cold
And gladly for brave Phillip
He came home with two golds.

SMILEY TILY

Smiley Tily, the lipstick Queen
The most glamorous woman I've ever seen
Her pithy one-liners keep us all entertained
But why is she limping? She looks in such pain
She's fallen, again, from her bike I assume
She's a danger to all but she certainly blooms
In her eye-catching costumes, such pretty attire
Her swimming not great but she's known as a trier
Post swim, what's this? Is that a rat on a string?
It's her darling dog Dasha, she's a funny looking thing
With Diane, Dawn, Helen, Clare, Lucy and Sue
Don't forget sister Jane, what a wonderful crew
She's blessed with charisma and an elegant style
The Queen of the lake makes our visits worthwhile.

TOO COLD FOR ME

The water's way too cold for me
I'm sadly not that brave
Once September has been and gone
I'll make my goodbye wave

The people, I admire them all
But I cannot compete
I'm frightened I might get cold hands
A frozen head and feet

They say it's good for mental health
I don't believe that's true
The cold makes me feel terrible
The experts have no clue

I could invest in neoprene
Some boots and a wetsuit
A pair of gloves for my cold hands
Could that approach bear fruit?

Some people say I'm way too soft
That I should grow a pair
But if I swam, then afterwards
My pair might not be there

The Wim Hof gang can have their fun
Forgive me for my snub
You might find joy submerged in ice
But I won't join your club

Perhaps I'll meet you afterwards
For coffee and some cake
But no chance that you'll see me swim
Not in that freezing lake

I won't get in the water
No, not for anything
Enjoy the ice-cold winter
I'll see you in the spring.

NAUGHTY SALLY TWINKLE

A sunny day, the lake's been drained
The Warriors felt glum
Where can they swim? The tide is in!
A sea swim then, please come
But with no wall to swim along
Close to the shore they'll stay
Row gave them all a safety talk
You must do as I say.

But Sally wasn't listening
She set off for the pier
So naughty, so ill disciplined
So, brave she knew no fear
Forgetting Row's number one rule
To never swim alone
And always swim with a tow float
A whistle and a phone

But Sally she was far away
She got to the fifth leg
No one around to rescue her
She sank to the seabed
All of a sudden, Row appeared
Towed Sally back to shore
So, Sally lived for other days
Her twinkle soon restored.

Oh, naughty Sally, silly girl
So lucky to be alive
Without Row's help and safety skills
You may not have survived
The Warriors were furious
But their anger was well meant
So thankful Row had rescued her
Sally's fiver was well spent.

THE CLEVEDON EEL

Deep in my burrow, I am safe from the world
Surrounded by mud at the foot of the lake
As the swimmers pass over and I watch them float by
Unaware of the presence of this watery snake
I might venture outside to explore in the murk
Maybe brush on a leg or an arm on my way
Though I keep, for the most part, myself to myself
When I feel under threat, in my burrow I'll stay

Until one day, around me, my whole world falls apart
The lake disappearing, where it's gone, I don't know
I flee from my burrow to the deep end I race
I am chasing the tide in this fast deathly flow
A whole gang of eels there are gathered as one
Where a puddle remains, in the depths by the wall
Our ending seems certain with no chance of escape
Though we're flapping and fighting, death awaits one and
all

Then appearing from nowhere there's a glimmer of hope
With a Twinkle we're saved from a cold, muddy grave
Flung into nature's bucket, full of water and life
Though our feelings uncertain in this foreign enclave
Then we're lifted up high as the seagulls prepare
In our vulnerable state, our fear grows at this sight
Till we're thrown in the channel, now we're safe from their
glare
In the darkness below we can sense a new light

Deep down on the seabed, we make burrows below
We need time to explore our new home in the sea
So, I play through the day out of sight, out of mind
Let loose in my new world, I feel safe, I feel free
But unknown to me, there are threats all around
In the silt I am blinded as I'm swept to the pier
Where a fishy treat tempts, then I'm trapped on the line
Oh bugger! I'm captured, seems my end could be near

Then I rise in the sky, to the top of the world
Soon the fisherman's supper? Left awaiting my fate
To the end of the line where the fisherman's pail
Sits so close, why on earth was I fooled by his bait?
Then out of nowhere, the Twinkle returns
There she pushes my captor to the water below
Where he makes a big splash and I'm free to escape
Once again, she has saved me, on my way I shall go

So, I'm back in the sea, yet another close shave
Now the current has turned, and I'm forced back
downstream
Back to where it all started, like I've not been away
As I'm carried back home, was it all a bad dream?
With the tide overtopping, I'm swept over the wall
With the waters replenished, I feel like I've returned
Back to where I belong, to my own home, sweet home
Where I'm safe in the water with new life lessons learned

PAUL

If you've ever seen an old man
Take a tumble in the lake
And you don't believe in what you saw
I can promise, it's not fake

If you hear a loud splash, then a cheer
The next time you're about
Then you've sadly missed him falling in
Of that, there is no doubt

At times he'll fall in backwards
Or he may land on his side
Or he'll make it look as if he's slipped
He won't let it hurt his pride

Sometimes you'll see him from the beach
Bravely climbing up the pier
As you watch him fall into the sea
You will see he has no fear

So, if you ever see him
Falling off of the pontoon
Say hi, then ask for his advice
You, too, could be tumbling soon.

GAV

You may see a cheeky fella
With his bike down at the lake
If you pop down now, he'll be there
He'll have been there since daybreak
He is normally found chatting
What a lovely, friendly guy
But he won't be in the water
He's the wonderful Gav Pri

Be prepared when you're conversing
He could quickly disappear
But he's neither rude nor tactless
And he's not gone for a beer
For his jobs to chase the dogs off
If he sees one on his patch
Don't you dare try to outsmart him
Or your mutt will meet its match

He can spot a dog from miles off
Once he sees one, he's possessed
Some consider him a loony
Some consider him obsessed
But for me our Gav's a hero
We must give him his fair due
If it wasn't for his courage
Our lake would be full of poo.

WENDY'S BIRTHDAY

The Walruses and Orcas
They met at last as friends
The in fighting was over
The troubles at an end
For Wendy was an Orcrus
So, loved by everyone
And as it was her birthday
They met up for some fun

A time for celebration
The lido booked all day
Okay, just for the morning
But lots of time to play
The invites had insisted
They all don fancy dress
And Paul chose his mankini
The ladies were impressed

Time for a Tebay tumble
Paul climbed out what a sight
On tumbling in he popped out
Gave one and all a fright
Paul, please stay in the water
Poor Wendy was enraged
This is meant to be my party
I shouldn't be upstaged

Once everyone recovered
It was time to play some sport
Some races, water polo
But Wendy cut it short
Enough of these shenanigans
These games are really dumb
Instead let's swim through Paul's legs
And emerge out of his bum

So, when the game was over
They climbed out feeling blessed
Wendy looked so beautiful
In her brand new mermaid dress
An array of cakes and flapjacks
An award for Tebay's thong
On Wendy's Happy Birthday
Thanks for all coming along.

JUNE'S BIRTHDAY BASH

I'm sixty-nine today said June, let's meet up at the lake
For next year I'll be way too old, we'll celebrate with cake
So, June she turned up for a swim, Alan and Ted in tow
But was Ted welcome at the lake? Nobody seemed to know

But why was Alan full of joy? He couldn't hide his smile
Did someone mention sixty-nine? With that June ran a mile
You daft fool, sixty nine's my age, you dirty, pervy man
But maybe when we get back home, if you are good, we can

So, as they swam around the lake, the joy was on June's face
She loved a swim with all her friends and more so in this place
Back on the side she looked around and gave a tactful cough
I need a hand please anyone, can someone pull me off?

So, with her wetsuit top removed, attentions turned to food
Gav smelt the bacon from his house, he thought it would be rude
To not attend June's birthday bash, he rode down on his bike
But on arrival he saw something which he didn't like

Oh, get that thing away from me, no horses allowed here
Can you not read the signs you fools? They make it very clear
Not true said June it says no dogs, no one will ban my Ted
If you don't like it bugger off, go somewhere else instead

Regrettably Gav's angry rage, was not for long suppressed
Whilst cake and bacon sandwiches were shared by all the guests
Gav opted for a dip instead, to make his swim debut
But when he got out of the lake his clothes were drenched with poo

Oh, good boy Ted, June full of pride, it serves him bloody right
If he decides to pick on you, we're ready for a fight
But Gav's anger had turned to smiles, just what was going wrong?
This shit will do my garden good, I love that pooey pong

With all the food and drink consumed, was time to bade farewell
And also, all the friends were keen to flee the shitty smell
So, June and Alan rode Ted home, June had a lovely day
Oh Alan, you've behaved for once, now have your wicked way.

THE MOLLY JOLLY

The Molly Jolly was here at last
The friends all hoping for a blast
The destination was Penarth
For Molly's brownies and plenty of laughs

The friends all gathered at the beach
No sign of Molly or her treats
Then Stephen saw her and ran for a hug
But not with Molly, with the brownies tub

Molly was seething, leave the brownies alone
These are for afterwards, once you have shown
That you can swim to the pier and back
Those who fail will not get a snack

This is Keri, she will be your guide
Where it's safe to swim she will decide
Keri spoke, please avoid the pier end
Those fishermen are not our friends

The current against them on the way
But with big efforts they crossed the bay
As they reached the pier it was time to relax
The current took them all the way back!

But where were Tim, Jo and Mary Nutley?
They weren't with the gang, were they lost at sea?
Then abruptly Jo Laird screamed out in horror
They're heading for the end of the pier, oh bother!

They're heading for the fishing lines
Cried Karen Brown, they'll get a fine
But a worse fate awaited the suicide squad
As Tim felt a hook around his knob

I've got a little un, the fisherman said
I'll pull him up from the seabed
He's actually bigger than I first thought
It's a fish with a beard, that's the first one I've caught

Oh no, screamed Lynnette, they're swimming away
Cheeky buggers said Molly, they're spoiling my day
I don't think it's deliberate said Posh Camilla
We need to do something or they'll drown in the river

Then out of nowhere Chris Rodgers appeared
Late as usual of course but full of ideas
The kids can form a chain out to sea
Then Billy can save them, I hope we agree

Well, the kids all thought it sounded such fun
So, with no time to lose the chain was begun
With the munchkins and triplets and Rosie and Jack
They had soon formed a chain, there was no turning back

Grab hold of Rosie, shouted Claire from the shore
But do it quickly, they can't hold on much more
With all holding tight, Billy pulled them to land
Thanks to Chris's quick thinking, it all went as planned

Thank heavens now we're all safe and sound
We can tuck into brownies, shall we pass them around?
But what about Tim? mentioned Jo Cheek and Stella
He's stuck on the pier with that fisherman fella

So, the friends they ventured towards the pier
Stopping first for an ice cream and a few pints of beer
Once there, they found Tim in a fisherman's pail
He was heavily guarded, any rescue would fail

It's ok, cried Jackie, I have a great plan
I'll flash my nice boobs at the fisherman
Then when he's spellbound by my lovely chest
Pete can save Tim if he tries his best

So, with the fisherman hypnotised
Pete and the others were able to prise
Tim out of the bucket, no more need for alarm
And finally, all the friends safe from harm

With everybody back on the beach
The friends were ready for their treats
Thank goodness everyone was safe and sound
Here's the brownies said Molly, I'll pass them around.

A TRIBUTE TO HER MAJESTY

The whole world was devastated about the sad death Of Her Majesty in 2022. We all have our favourite memories of her and her wonderful dresses. My favourite story about the Queen is the one about her visit to Clevedon in 1979.

Her Majesty was visiting Clevedon to open something or other and, afterwards, she attended a lunch in the Sailing Club. Local dignitaries and celebrities invited included the celebrated bowls player, David Bryant. Also on the guest list was Gertrude Higginbottom. Many of you will remember that Gertrude holds the record for the longest Pier to Ladye Bay swim which she completed an incredible twenty-two times. Gertrude recalls,

"Obviously I was delighted to meet Her Majesty. Once the small talk was complete, I expected her to move on to the next guest but, to my surprise, she told me she was a lover of open water swimming and she was well aware of my exploits. She told me it was one of her long held ambitions to complete the pier to Ladye Bay swim and she was wondering if I would accompany her as she thought it unsafe to swim alone. Obviously, I could not refuse such an offer and, after checking tide times on my phone (by sheer luck it was due to be high tide in one hour), we set off on the walk to Ladye Bay.

I remember being very jealous that she was able to walk up to Ladye Bay in her dryrobe. It was a wet and windy day and I would have relished the extra warmth mine provided. There was no way I could have squeezed my dryrobe into my tow float though, so I had to leave it in the cave and manage without it. Her Majesty, though, was able to hand her dryrobe to one of her butlers when we arrived at Ladye Bay and he was able to run back to the pier beach with it so that it would be there waiting for her on her return.

We entered the water as the tide turned and had a lovely heads up breaststroke swim as far as the hotel. Obviously, I am unable to reveal full details of our conversation. Her Majesty though, did speak of her love of open water swimming which she had inherited from her mother. She also spoke of how her mother had told her the story of Betty and Mildred as a child and how it had been her ambition to emulate Mildred's achievement ever since (minus the death bit).

As we passed the hotel, Her Majesty suddenly told me she would race me to the pier. This put me in an awkward position. Obviously, I couldn't beat her but I also didn't want to be seen as patronising her by letting her win. I needn't have worried though as, even swimming flat out, I was unable to keep up with her. She had a wonderful front crawl technique. It was only later I discovered that she was on course to represent Great Britain in the Olympics in 1948 until she picked up a shoulder injury weeks before the games were due to begin.

As we arrived at the beach, I remember the shock of seeing a number of corgis running to the water's edge to greet her. As we all know, dogs are banned from the pier beach but nobody was going to argue with The Queen. I remember a young faced Gav Pri was in attendance that day. He didn't look happy but even he wasn't going to tell Her Majesty the corgis weren't welcome.

Once we were dried off and were back in our dryrobes, I was offered a cup of tea. I politely declined as I had not brought a cup. Her Majesty said that wouldn't be a problem as she always had her china tea set with her. To this day, this remains the only time I have had my post swim drink from a cup and saucer. I was also offered cucumber sandwiches (with the crusts cut off) and a slice of Victoria sponge (especially poignant given we were swimming to honour the exploits of Betty and Mildred in Victorian times).

Sadly, Her Majesty was unable to hang around as she had to dash off to Yatton to open some orphanage or donkey sanctuary or something. I bade her a fond farewell. That day will live in my memory forever."

This excerpt is taken from Gertrude Higginbottom's unpublished autobiography, Twenty-Two Ways. Thanks to her Granddaughter Olivia, for allowing me to share this story.

I wrote this poem to celebrate the platinum Jubilee of Her Majesty, just a few months before her sad end.

HER MAJESTY

Her Majesty resplendent
In her beautiful blue dress
What a wonderful ambassador
Always dresses to impress
Whether waving to her people
Paying visits to the ill
Never seen without a smile
What a destiny fulfilled
Always dignified and regal
She is loved by one and all
With her corgis and her horses
Holds her subjects in her thrall
As we celebrate her Jubilee
Let's remember how she's served
For the UK, God and Commonwealth
All the plaudits well deserved.

A FEW OTHER POEMS

THE BULLY

He who always knows best
Mister Perfect, King of the obscene
Don't cross him, don't upset him
Make sure your kitchen's clean
Those who feel his wrath
Rarely live to tell the tale
Without his support and approval
You'll be doomed, destined to fail
His vitriol turns the air blue
Abuse leaves morale destroyed
A persona to sell to the Devil?
Or a loathsome bully deployed?
Their misery unheeded
When it boosts his power and fame
To humiliate, to vilify
His one and only aim.

PARTYGATE

Sick on the floor and wine on the wall
They lie to the country, they lie to us all
The late night parties, the cases of booze
The pizza, prosecco, the wild leaving dos
The brawls and the quizzes, the vomit and cake
I hope poor old Boris was not kept awake
The cheese and the wine, the back garden packed
The one person absent, the only one sacked
Away from this shambles, no mixing outside
No meet ups with friends, that pleasure denied
No goodbyes to loved ones, no chance to hold hands
They die all alone, compassion is banned
Apologies half-baked, their duty ignored
They tell us to move on, they're all getting bored
All sanctions evaded, their words all untrue
Please do as they say, don't do as they do.

DEATH OF A LIAR

The Black Knight is shameless as he drowns in his mire
Digging deeper and deeper whilst the nations on fire
A pitiful failure, corrupt to the end
Holds the keys to the office but a foe, not a friend
He's brazen, yet spineless, on self-loathing he thrives
As the lies grow in number, he feels more alive
To save his own skin he leaves Britain to burn
No love for the country, that's not his concern
The lies they engulf him and all that we know
Barefaced in his smugness, he is forced to let go
The people applaud the demise of this cheat
A slow, painful death, now disgraced in defeat.

IN TRUSS WE TRUST

We're all in agreement, in Truss we trust
She'll save this fine nation from going bust
She's full of compassion, we know that she cares
She's up front and honest, without any airs
Her confidence glows, as bold as brass
With an eye for detail and a touch of class
Impressive and competent whenever she speaks
The cheers are so loud, they last for weeks
Inspiring such loyalty from one and from all
Acclaimed and feted, she stands so tall
Liz pays no favour to the rich
Equality her founding pitch
Respect observed from far and wide
Whoever you are, she's on your side
We're all behind her every step of the way
She boosts Britain's standing every day
No chance this great country could ever combust
Not with Liz in command, in Truss we trust.

I WON'T BE WATCHING

I won't be watching, the bribes were not mine
I won't be seen towing, their corrupt party line
These oil fuelled riches, they come at a price
I will pay no heed to their sordid advice
To respect, to ignore, to not get involved
To enjoy the show and leave FIFA absolved
To ignore Qatar's failings on human rights
To turn a blind eye when reality bites
To pretend migrant slaves were not left to die
It's amazing with FIFA, what money can buy
Their attempts to whitewash, inhuman and cruel
Demanding the players and the fans play the fool
No surprise to see FIFA soiling their bed
When profit means far more than any bloodshed
So, I won't be watching, but what if you do?
Well, what can I say? Then, that's up to you.

KEVIN AND LEANDER

This was written for the wedding of two of my friends but, sadly, I was not allowed to read it out during the service.

I've never liked Leander
To this day that remains true
So why am I at this wedding?
I honestly don't have a clue
She's the cloud which blocks the sun out
She's the rain which spoils our day
She's the wind which knocks us over
As for Kevin- he's ok
Oh Kevin, you can't dislike Kevin
Does he know what life has in store?
A lifetime wed to Leander
A lifetime of blood and gore
She's the serpent who entices
He's the victim of deceit
She's the lion with the fierce roar
He's the sheep without the bleat
Oh Kevin, poor, poor Kevin
I feel for him today
But as he seems to love her
Let us bless them on their special day.

LOUISE AND THE SNOWMAN

Louise made a Snowman on Christmas Eve
But silly Louise, she was rather naive
She thought that the Snowman would come to life
She thought he would ask her to be his wife
But the Snowman was silent and still in the night
It felt like her Snowman would never take flight
But that morning she woke, and the Snowman seemed
real
He was walking and talking and was able to feel
That Louise was so precious, and he had a new friend
In the magic of Christmas, they were able to spend
The day flying high, with the Snowman her guide
Then he asked her, that night, if she'd be his bride
So, Louise felt so happy, she slept well in her bed
But when she woke the next morning, the poor Snowman
was dead

SCONE OR SCONE

For years we've all wondered
Is it scone? Is it scone?
But despite all the quarrels
The answer's unknown
Some insist it's a scone
Others claim it's a scone
There's no chance of agreement
With no facts to call on

In Cornwall it's settled
That the jam's the first thrown
On the top of the scone
Or on top of the scone?
Whilst in Devon, they tell us
That the cream is first on
But the county divided
If it's scone or it's scone

With so many great choices
What's our favourite scone?
Plain or cheesy or fruity?
All delicious, soon gone
But debate still it rages
Is it scone? Is it scone?
There's no solving this puzzle
As this poem has shown

SOMEONE TOOK MY BISCUITS

Someone took my biscuits
I don't know what to do
I moaned but no one listened
Who can I complain to?

I left them here the other day
I won them fair and square
Now I'm sad and hungry
And no one seems to care

I wish I knew who ate them
Just for my peace of mind
I'm broken, they're not coming back
Those thieves, they're so unkind

The police cannot be bothered
About my missing treat
They say it's not important
I'm giving up, I'm beat

Last night I dreamt I found them
And shared them with my chums
But when I woke, I realised
There was just a pile of crumbs

And now my tummy's empty
No biscuits means no hope
What can I do? I'm sick of this
I don't know how I'll cope

I'm lost without my biscuits
I just can't carry on
If only I'd remembered
To take them, now they're gone

CHEESE

In Wallace and Gromit, there's a moon made of cheese
Far too much cheese to eat, it could lead to unease
With our arteries blocked, we will splutter and wheeze
Lead to coronary failure or, perhaps, heart disease.

To preserve this much cheese, we will need space to
freeze
All the cheese in a freezer, will you buy me one please?
One the size of the moon, do they make one of these?
We could eat it forever, maybe with cheesy peas.

Pungent, stinky like feet, that's my fantasy cheese
Served with biscuits and fruit, what a thought, what a
tease
Goes so well with the honey which is made by the bees
We'll enjoy it outside, in the shade of the trees.

Once we've eaten it all, it will be such a squeeze
To fit into our trousers, we'll be down on our knees
Constipated, we'll find that life isn't a breeze
When we've stuffed ourselves full of this beautiful cheese.

THE CAT

Devious trickster
Sleek and slender
Cold and elusive
Warm and tender

Brutal butcher
Mild and carefree
Selfish and vicious
Soft and cuddly

Shameless, undignified
Proud and upstanding
Lonesome not lonely
Lazy, demanding

Biter, scratcher
Often goes missing
Turns up guilt free
So dismissing

Evil, loving
Killer, doting
Cruel but cosy
Watch her gloating

Loves you? hates you?
Couldn't care less?
What's her verdict?
What's your best guess?

Printed in Great Britain
by Amazon

20016996R00068